"Expansive.... [Ari] Banias's chief strength as a poet lies in observation.... In this memorable work, Banias offers readers a guide to seeing the world, and its incongruences, more clearly." —*Publishers Weekly*

"Ari Banias's poetry sits in an abandoned chair under the overpass, atop an 'oil slick on the Aegean' looking 'at, not through' reality's immeasurables ... holding it all in mind so we can also hold it.... The paper antiquity of deli coffee cups and 'A doric column / squatting in a strip mall' and 'the discotheque / painted tourist pink with a classical name' evoke the churn of some perpetual history whose action-reaction is embodied in the motion of lyrical meter and the news reports this book takes apart. The poet calls it 'A yellow butterfly that has no interest in me. / I have no interest in kings.' Such cosmic foreshortening disembarrasses the poem from imperial valence until all that's left of the book is 'just the tree.' When Ari Banias says 'don't be sorry for the future sand / this stone wall will become' one can almost let it go. Almost."
—Ana Božicevic, author of *JOMO*

"If every book of poetry, from now until the end—or the terminal twisting—of time were to offer itself as a field guide to the apocalypse by attrition in which we are living, in which we are forcing each other to live, then I would nominate Ari Banias's *A Symmetry* to be among the books that we consult first. In its clear and capacious inventory of the inter- and codependence of what feels like the fullness and failing of all things, Banias's poetry is transcribing a kind of vigilance that is mournful yet magnetizing, altruistic yet self-adhesive, and always enflowered by the daily uprising of new manifestations of love."
—Brandon Shimoda, author of *The Grave on the Wall*

"In *A Symmetry*, Ari Banias attunes to unacquainted frequencies with great precision and extraordinary craft, gauging the flow, intensity, and impact of sensuality, alternating between brutal excesses and incalculable joys. Every line holds. Reading this book is like feeling gravity. One walks unaware of the pull until the incline's encounter."

—Gregg Bordowitz, author of *Volition* and *Tenement*

"The surge, the swell, and the casual mutability of the borders and breaks that ensconce our world are laid bare in *A Symmetry*, Ari Banias's incandescent new collection of poems. . . [H]is work comes alive at the edges, the thresholds, and the charged moment where distance can finally collapse. . . . Near the end of *A Symmetry*, Banias ropes 'a brief fish / netted / partly recovered / the sweat of a horse / the wet of its eye.' These objects are momentarily linked and next time we see them, their potential will likely be revealed in an entirely new arrangement. This is one way to see—what taut instructions Banias has given us."

—Asiya Wadud, author of *No Knowledge Is Complete Until It Passes Through My Body*

"These poems are a talisman I want to wear around my neck, an eye that wards off evil by looking at what's before it with unflinching commitment and devotion. Awake to possibility and care in the half-light of our belated era, they give this reader shelter from 'the structures crumbling' around us. Bursting with energy and attention and love, this book offers us the world." —Eleni Sikelianos, author of *Your Kingdom*

A SYMMETRY

ALSO BY ARI BANIAS

Anybody

A SYMMETRY

POEMS

ARI BANIAS

W. W. NORTON & COMPANY

Celebrating a Century of Independent Publishing

For information about permission to reproduce selections from this book, write to
Permissions, W. W. Norton & Company, Inc., 500 Fifth Avenue, New York, NY 10110

For information about special discounts for bulk purchases, please contact
W. W. Norton Special Sales at specialsales@wwnorton.com or 800-233-4830

Manufacturing by Lakeside Book Company
Production manager: Beth Steidle

Library of Congress Cataloging-in-Publication Data

Names: Banias, Ari, author.
Title: A symmetry : poems / Ari Banias.
Description: First edition. | New York : W. W. Norton & Company, [2021]
Identifiers: LCCN 2021025184 | ISBN 9780393868135 (hardcover) |
ISBN 9780393868142 (epub)
Subjects: LCGFT: Poetry.
Classification: LCC PS3602.A6365 S96 2021 | DDC 811/.6—dc23
LC record available at https://lccn.loc.gov/2021025184

ISBN 978-1-324-06452-7 pbk.

W. W. Norton & Company, Inc., 500 Fifth Avenue, New York, N.Y. 10110
www.wwnorton.com

W. W. Norton & Company Ltd., 15 Carlisle Street, London W1D 3BS

1 2 3 4 5 6 7 8 9 0

CONTENTS

1

2

3

4

1

ORACLE

I was wrong it isn't

suffering that's easy pleasure that's difficult

How is it I have been living this way

holding my piss

a mirror scuffed by distant talk, secretly livid

worried what the dead would think?

Someone greets with only the top half of her head

brown curly hair behind a computer monitor

Today for one second a woman is anyone who has a body

and can't forget it

The tight loops of the office carpet start to unhook

Some men are women too

the way a mountain is land and a harbor is land and a parking lot

Refuse the difference between sameness and difference

The ocean is on fire

green flame on the neck of a god

who is a pile of rocks

not apologizing for themselves

QUALM

Iridescent green flies on the dog shit scatter when I walk by.

I've never seen flies so vivid. Gorgeous, these shit-flies.

Someone sits on a park bench with head in hands.

A plot of ornamental grass bends in resigned unison.

Helicopters overhead, how they move

like spirits with no conscience.

Patience. Rage and being told "be patient."

The birds with orange heads and dust-colored bodies bob on the power
lines.

The poet explains *a patient* is "one who suffers."

Beneath the highway underpass, a chair overturned in the fenced-in
weeds

toward which a misplaced tenderness arises.

Each night, she says, and most mornings, refugees arrive.

Then ship off to Athens. Why would they want to stay, there's nothing
here.

Fog descended from the Pacific;

I took a bath with my biggest rock. A deity,

ancient, severe, rolling around in the bottom of the tub.

———————

Nothing: a bookstore, a lotto place run by cousins, two bakeries, one

university, donated

used baby clothes well-meaningly folded and stacked, one

detention center in the capital

road sign with the capital's distance in kilometers spray painted FUCK

———————

Where one bright aperture in the cloud has closed up

inner tubes and shoes and life vests flare on the shore.

My mother lives above this beach. She watches them.

———————

After being asked for money by five separate people

an office supply truck passes with GIVE SOMETHING BACK across it.

I give five dollars to Ceci.

I gave two dollars to someone earlier, but he seemed disappointed.

I sit on a sunny curb in the parking lot, feeling useless, like a teenager.

Ha, who is American! my mother asks bitterly.

One of us looks down at the other.

Palm tree in the distance with the hair of a rocker dude.

———————

My mother said fight.

She said they used to call her "the little Spañola."

———————

Photographs of water, like case studies.

How far away from yourself would you say you get?

When I swim the first time, I cannot call the feeling pleasure.

———————

"Them" here feels violent to me.

———————

Three kids in the chilly light

of a convenience store's back entrance

visible from the highway

between one California and another.

One squats looking at a phone,

two lean and smoke.

Slouch of interminable suburbia

interminable crap-jobs at fifteen

a flash, momentary as toward the city

we continue. As we do.

———————

Four old paint drips

on the windowpane I look

at, not through.

Four old punctuation marks

a nearing helicopter cuts across.

I refuse to detail the humiliations that keep me up at night.

I am pulling a blanket over my head.

Or, I'm elated by 30 seconds of rain.

—————————

At the laundromat

churchlike, fastidiously polite,

I pair socks at the high counter,

plastic marbled to resemble marble

black, white, and blue.

A woman claims a whole row of washers

spacing five hefty trash bags

at even intervals, looking tired.

Here our delicates.

I sit down she gets up.

A stranger I want to convey kindness to.

The day opens like a compact,

mirror on one side

powder on the other.

PRACTICE

I try to hold in my mind
a chemical fire in Texas
a chemical explosion in Yancheng
a passage by rubber boat from Kuşadası to Vathy
without even the before or the after
as though discreet
as I can hold
the mad king going madder
the spotless meeting room
a team of lawyers
the hemorrhoids of a team of lawyers
the soothing creams
each purchased individually or
the parched fields
I have in my view
a pink bucket on its side in the garden all winter
a barely contained moment of ecstasy
on a golf course stomping hard with my boots
on spongy treated earth
Julie fucking Andrews / I shout into the high winds
toward a brown scribble of unmanicured woods
gales from the west southwest
the thousands of second homes standing empty
swamps from which the spotted salamanders emerge after thaw
after how many gallons of fuel in enormous steel tanks
arrive at their destination intact
what can it possibly mean to remain intact
to oppose smug minimalism
what can the
22,000 metric tons of trash entering the ocean today

in the bloodstream
in the paperwork
in the partially masked
resentments in any work
forced in the corn in the soy
in the wheat / I try to hold in my mind
as I hold in my mind
a white van and an ATV
yellow as a 90s Sony Walkman
the chocolate milk stain
birthmark on your right inner thigh
right next to your pussy like a witness
glossy ivy climbing the trees
having snared a single gray shopping bag
tattered spirit
bird again in the exhaust vent making its nest
my fingers in you
and your face while I do that
mythic and ancient face of centuries
comedy tragedy
microplastics buried imperceptibly in
the face I can't completely / hold the
face I love

PORTAL

Every weekend someone wants to cut grass

put out a painted chest of drawers

without the drawers

that raw interior

The mole below your left eye,

an amber planet, glows

I told you field of flowers

but a book about patterns says dots

first meant the plague, then conformity, then irreverence

Can't lacquer a pit

A swimming pool inner blue but mossing

at its edge—irresist—I watch you

take shape in

You gone

Cold fingers to surround a cup

warm milk to think in

The word cruelty is absolutely perfect

As if dropped from a plane

a white poodle tumbles through the sky

and lands in a city river a swan

Woman in Lemat says to me "Your smile is beautiful

I hope you keep it"

a law against refugees

passed by the children of refugees

decorative hellenic borders

on deli coffee cups

on a silver ring I used to wear

it feels nationalist now

/it was always nationalist

actually I would say dawn is fruity

not milky, not gold

what to do with the lie of ethnicity

at dinner T says

"Greece" is an invention

of the nineteenth century

set on a plinth

was this green once? unknown

the cicadas go on

I had a body and it was good
until you gave it meaning.
Meaning ruined pleasure
and created it
so ruin creates
and pleasure's meaning
I didn't ask for just lived through
a gate that shrieked each time
it opened and on the street
we passed one another
flicking our eyes at then away from
the bodies made boring
by the small clamors that drown out
the one large clamor.
Something in the tree is arguing with the tree?
No that's just the tree.

THREE TONGUES

The first one died
licking sand thinking of the sea
split in three

The first a weed resembling
whoever's nearest
its medicines camouflaged
in mimesis

The second was a bankrupt
study abroad program
with a sentimental little nationalist streak
A doric column
squatting in a strip mall
The fragrant mountain ringed in castoff
first world nouns

That it was written
That it is understood
But how to describe the third

The taste of water . . . ?
Paradox?

The third is
using my desire
to save from the force of desire
a turquoise burro meant for smashing
I mean to hold

A word that looks at you
as if it knows you
and you feel warm

the room you back into
while staring directly at a light source
so now you twitch

without hearing the command to twitch

the sweat x the slabs x the proportions
the sun's calculable angle x hours chiseled
the subtraction of color x bootlicking oaths
honey x the accent's placement x mourning clothes
tired comparisons x the carrying it forward
x centuries balancing it on her heads x
the grief-sellers x the followers
x the rapist minor gods x
buttery calfskin ripped from its cry x aging protégés
x soft but not quite pretty enough boys x
democracy launderers x shit-shovelers x deathless kings
the lips x the pits x tender cunts of every iteration
scouring rags x candle dippers x elastic scrotal skin
bottomless refills x back to normal x the strays cropped out
clotted tongues x factory farmed embarrassed poets x scale replicas
the package tour x sculpted wastewater channel x hypotenuse
inclusion x inexhaustible lazy olive branch motifs
the pre recorded oracle x brutality with slicker PR
bacterial feasts x the stream of piss
running into the water stream x coercion
mistaken for touch x cocksucking for docility
the drape x the folds x didactic plaques
x the worship of walls x an exact middle
the reader x the tourist x the sell-by date
detention camp x gag order x garbage strike
the shattered phone x pottery shard x flaming cheese
immortal x ostracized x dawn
the width x the length x the weight
pity x hierarchy x calculated exchange x
heroic death x a greased loophole x the sucked braid

FOUNTAIN

You recount the history of the French garden.

From above, I see tight rows of trees beside threadbare grass.

When the language teacher talks about le capitalisme:

the gesture of three fingers rubbing imaginary fabric.

I'm a tourist, vulnerable and stupid,

my legs showing, shoes practical, face red.

Together, we try to reconstruct an anecdote

whose contents have scattered. A motorcycle passes, a French police siren

you say sounds innocuous then we both laugh sourly.

I hadn't seen a woman slap a child in some time.

A truck reversing, and the alarm that continues for hours one morning.

Porn on a handheld device, its tinny echo in a room

with bare floors and very little furniture.

Across the courtyard, this T-shirt on a hanger out the window

turns in the light breeze as if trying to look behind itself.

I'm consumed with not knowing where to buy paper, safety pins, stamps.

The window frames of that building are red, emerging from gray gables.

Enormous bumblebee at the threshold investigates the doorway,
    doesn't enter.

The flies do; they're promiscuous; they leave.

I don't know the word for because.

So each act is disconnected from another.

I can almost imagine there are no consequences,

the days just pass, one sunny, one cloudy, someone unseen shouts, sirens

every few hours, clouds move in a solemn procession across

a wide sky staggered with chimneys,

people wait to cross the street, a large tree tosses its wig a little.

Other small trees in the courtyard flicker.

They are responsive.

The sun heats the pavement; le pavé répond.

You send me a short erotic video, you're naked, propositioning me.

Do you act more like the coin or the water?

Across the narrow street this bird

sipping from roof puddles

seems more dove than pigeon.

Pacing, grandmotherly, she keeps stopping to look at me.

Do you just know how to love another person

like someone knew to paint those window frames red?

Most of the architecture looks floral, like a boring math problem.

The crosses reach and reach.

Why does the scrape of the furniture when I rearrange it

sound like crass American English to me?

I slept late, now I'm watching the clouds, like clouds

in an eighteenth-century painting. Overly articulate.

Except these clouds are not trying to symbolize anything.

Where's my dove.

I always want to go look at people.

A booth selling copies of copies of Louis Vuitton.

The small shadow the roof makes on another roof right next to it.

When my friend came to Paris she wanted to break everything.

Impeccable shoes on the impeccable feet.

Clothes so new they're creamy, and to seem to never have to
    compromise.

I feel tattered when I'm actually not;

I'm an American, I eat.

A huge decorative basket of citrus stationed beside me in the upscale
    bistro.

The woman from a building opposite comes down, indignant:

Who threw a pomelo into my window?

You read to me about the history of the barricade.

I picture the drab suburbs.

The shoulders and elbows of people in the museum evoke more reaction

in me than most of the paintings.

A young lithe person with live eyes tends bar, *gender trouble* tattooed
    up their arm.

I count twenty-nine sleeping bags lined up beneath the overhang

and each one inhabited.

I read to you about the history of enclosure.

Two people talking on a balcony, their black hair blowing.

One leaning over into the courtyard.

Behind the cathedral, vulgar black felt stapled into the raised flower beds

to mask their frames.

The river stinks, allures, as a specific person can.

A repository, a consequence, a long sentence, an ongoing story.

The generous current cut through by a party boat shouting

wooo! wooo! wooooooo! wooo!

emitting an obscene light

waving at whatever will wave back.

BLUE

Here the trees appear
pasted up against the side of it
in front of hills. Partly this has to do with light partly
with position.

Wanting a perceptual shift, stare up.
Against the side
of what has no sides

here in front of some hills with no front.

———————

What it feels to be; what you are told.

The stubborn programming.

———————

The single palm on the horizon
a shaggy lap dog. A figurine
on a mantel
waiting to be noticed or dusted . . .

———————

The highway's curve
is a thought someone had,

and we travel the shape
of that thought.

———————

Space junk, earth junk, human waste.
From here looks "empty" or "clean."

It's a matter of position.

Police helicopters, pilotless aircraft, satellites,
warplanes I don't know the names of.
The color deepens. Try to see this as a clarification.

—————————

Pacific grating the side of the bluff

Pacific we only touch like this

never arriving

—————————

A light in the distance. The idea of "the distance."

—————————

I put my hand on your leg to assure myself
of what?

—————————

These mountains appear to divide
something green from something yellow
something brown from something browner. Something grayish with
lines in it.

—————————

Multimillion-dollar homes small enough to crush under my thumb

I even love the gnats
was thinking this as I walked through a marsh marked Private Property
bordered by a six-lane road
with blocks of new construction
sandy orange, peachish-beige condos right
in the path of the sunset
later I was thinking I even like this long blond strand of hair
here beside the hotel pool caught on a rivet
fixed to the plywood lounging platform painted black
and faced in wood laminate so as to appear . . . stylish?
it's cheap
the wind blows a bit then settles
the hair flails energetically then almost vanishes
I count three separate hairs each claimed by a different screw
a single cloud passes over the sun
from another vantage the cloud would be elsewhere
gnats and birdsong ecstatic in the reeds
the lit up LA FITNESS sign reflected in the marsh water
white on liquid pink
a duck paddles across and the letters smear
LAST FINES
FASIL NEST
FAINTLESS
it can be some other way
and is

The magnolia before it blooms stands

bare as a statue from antiquity or

a shaved puss, it flowers first

then greens. A pissed off dyke

climbs into the branches

to be held by an ancient

indifference and both

were me. Yet it's possible I am

a short bald man. That I am neither

a big-bosomed wide-hipped pretty

nor a short bald man. An antelope, an elk, a deer

on this rug, a twiggy tree.

The genderless squat figure,

solo, blurry, hands on hips, that repeats.

A plush life of winter and

summer colors of flowers alongside

tight checkered bands

edging the broad green center

where we look for each other,

a woods, a pasture, a park, a yard, a median of grass

set in a concrete mold situated

within a pay lot. How it feels to stand

outside a house at night whose lights are on.

Whose lights are on.

2

fake real estate / real air space

where a hummingbird swerves at my red watch cap

not a flower

my eyes mouth face a conceptual flower

a breach in emotional security

time waged against a living wage

after a decade fifteen dollars / hour is not

my subject position   your subject position

in the ahistorical grassland   financial district stripped of

industrial zone "where no one lives"

seaside village "where no one lives"

the subjective field near the mountain where the gods make their
        decisions

where my friend visits each spring to gather herbs to make medicines

against the state to practice this medicine

privacy / piracy

she is there now   gathering

Accepting money from the rich   the water ruffles

keeping their boats afloat

sucking down fuel

nothing comes down to touch you

just have to know it's there

person in the bed of a truck looking out to the leafless trees

a long stubborn line of survivors   you need

the will to help each other continue   you need

knowing how to fix an engine, a skill for sweet talk

oh   have a question

is elegy pure mourning or is there room for the shit things he did

that you were forced & that so much of forcing does not appear

a hot plate for dinner and somewhere to sit

two colors of blue

pull back and what remains

what you put up with for somewhere to sit

climate-controlled corporate headquarters

UV blocking suicide-proof windows

"What did the o say to the 8?"

"Nice belt!"

The M in Monarch Plumbing and Heating wears a tilted crown

A green flower-shaped boat on the Mayflower shipping container

Across from the Nashua river not eternal

a Wendy's and a Kohl's not eternal

the itchy desolation of spring surrounds

the battered safety cone holding its shape

Frost's mending wall

A sign for Manifest Builders

once pain was quiet / now it instructs me

is pain the river

the paper mills concentrated along

flowing downstream

during the early colonial period

is it seized is it treated

is it subject to

industrial / scenic

does pain meet with the mayor

or reason with execs

under new management (same)

who oversees it

what does it restore

in whose nature is pain asking

what rivers

did this paper destroy

The wind took the almond tree the outer door the satellite dish

She squints at the brilliant water, repeats a story she already told

a hand closes two sets of blue shutters against day

She admits she's depressed—

terracotta tiles rest in their formal sequence

Build a home where no amount of money

could ever protect you

the blameless salt the raving sea

Athena's temple, scaffold-covered wreck

weeds with such roots no person can pull

To throw a rough

and glittering stone into the sea

and forget its individual qualities

Everyone young who can leaves for the city

A Volos cousin bought an olive grove to run a paintball field

He props old doors against the trees for cover

If it hurts to be struck he doesn't say

The uncle, farmhands, aunt

all look like men

The cafés full, meticulous gelled hair

Everyone smokes

flushed octopus hang drying

That truth is not cliché isn't true

Dad sends a pic of an olive tree 400 years old

it looks like any tree

the highest branches silver as they were

An ancient wall runs obscured by grass

along the top of that hill

Someone in a red skirt methodically beats the trees

with a heavy stick looks like any stick

People other people say are not from here

point out the path

To want to dissolve and be anything

crab grass Panera Bread

transmission fluid leaked onto a parking spot

compressed aluminum sheeting

new toilet in a flipped house

that old guy's tan baseball hat

with machine embroidered American flag on it

/ even that?

                            well

Half-exposed in a cheerful email

a half-clandestine meeting of underpaid workers

A cruelty of temperature and color

ice queen in heat

See iridescent motor oil on asphalt, think unicorn piss

planet earth at the end of a keychain

Danny put down his pants then handed over

a literalist   a little lamb

gay people not knowing other gay people are gay

unpaid mandatory lunch breaks

an ancient temple to the wind god discovered under a supermarket

I leave the word "discovered" / to let the pattern speak

I am listening   the apologizers now say

the judge wears a more ornate collar ruffle to signify disagreement

decorum / suggests the ruffle

decorum / doesn't want you feeling free

people not here

rush into the public squares

people in group therapy trade off

yelling at an empty chair

In the church courtyard

a prickly rope fixed to the bell

Starched embroidered guest pillowcases

on a mattress stuffed with raw wool

beneath a hammered metal crucifix

On the empty line rusty springs of clothespins

spin intermittent in wind

Scratched glass Fanta bottles filled and refilled

Gray-haired men at the coffee shop

sitting for half a century their hands at tables

dark suit pants and light shirts

Any woman at the coffee shop that kind of woman

As the watermelon-seller's battered truck

loudspeaker crackling makes its rounds

the slap of sandals on cement

the sun-stiffened sheet

a dark magenta flowering vine

spills over the high gate of the diplomat's house

To speak without vulnerability you claimed

impossible

the land's fragrance its honey its plants

translation   I wanted to be back in my language

"back"? /

I wanted to differently be in

another word for being

einai   eimai   estar

small brown moth frazzling the windowpane

another way

to live in the rind living had shed

Your spine's doing great the chiropractor says

that the source of the pain is a disconnection

she suspects self-protective

between heart / pelvis

"there is no communication"

between mind / ground

At my desk I swivel my hips in exaggerated circles

for three minutes

as if to undo lifetimes of this "no"

Where someone spraypainted ATHENS IS THE NEW BERLIN

the retort follows

BERLIN IS THE NEW ATHENS

on a billboard for instant coffee above the café

in the ardent sun

go ahead / wish for it

A creek running under the building / makes the walls sweat

the weedbro next door exhales directly into my apartment

whose cheap rent is triple

what Greek friends already can't afford

they scan the room and slam the door

of his housekeeper the American poet wrote "like a Palmyra matron /

Copied in lard and horsehair"

of everyone in language school I had the most believable accent

I can pretend to read coffee grounds

in lurching fragments

should I worry about this feeling?

blithe vacation photos in my feed

of a person who'd emailed asking

for interesting things to do in Athens

you're a stray dog, you don't know where you're from

we had the whole cove to ourselves

tourism is / to drink from one's cut

then again it depends

where you were in the '70s

your relationship to polyester blends

dictatorship

interminable queues

hospitality

the phrase "exhausted blue"

tar deposits on beaches

Someone wheels an empty wheelbarrow

past windows where two women fold sheets

in yellowish light / the white sheets

make shapes in the window as they work

triangle rectangle square

shapes I'm hungry for

Someone walks the other way / without the wheelbarrow

the sheets in a sizeable heap

at one end of the long table

their arms pass over

I want to resist a comparison

to healers but this is how their hands move

as they open / then fold something away

as they tend to it

She takes two corners taut

and shakes it down in one crisp move

lays it on the table where it settles

in time

brings the other two corners / to the first

to make the sheet disappear

Only one person folding now

behind three large windows and a tall white fan

which is off

I describe the shape of a plot of land

how its vegetation stirs in varying wind

the detritus gathered

at the foot of the fence   little garbage froth

the day's color   a building's texture

a fixed point in a landscape intimately

but not the menace of

a man with outrageous pants praising

a former head of state

his relation by marriage /

O love how do I find

the love of what is unloved

in this man

or whose job is this

mine?

At 4 am the nightbirds calling 18, 18, 18

in translation the syllables

for the number

sound stingy

rationalism, reason

its off-season scaffolds

its bleed edge

"imagine the whole country is a museum . . .

every little stone" imperial

pictures of food bigger than the actual food

on loan,

as a favor, a tourist fingers

and considers a green piece of sea glass

with interest

then tosses it back

from a Heineken you or I could have

chugged in the 90s

smooth as a youth's ass

it hurts to smack into genre

willingly maintained

linty remnant in the research funding

compliant / complaint

the project of attention being

a large percentage of looking away-from

I'm to remain rare   by becoming example

for example the hall without windows

or air I come to feel comfortable in

then *come to* /

theoretically sorry as the window

a bird takes for sky

and unattainable as a corner office

if I refuse to perforate or divide

You like the smell of the air here   it feels right

What a thing to say   my body said it

air traveling in and out of the lungs

Old people are visible here   it feels right

tangible as wool

when shepherds are not abstract

events mediated through a screen

If it's visible on screen, that's not your body

visible in the coffee grounds if it's the future

If it is, it smells like the room

right before she sees what their

rifle butts have done

There's no word for events just life

as it shrinks   enlarging

one gold coin

and then it's spent

A train horn in the distance

sounding mournful   frantic

or resigned

like someone at the end of the day

saying ach panagia mou

unrolling the stockings from her legs

for the 25,000th time

3

The beauty of my home
is that it moves

is how the thinking goes

70 years ago my grandfather trades a gold bracelet for an egg

A salt particle from the volcanic boulders
dissolves
reconstitutes

into terraces footpaths little heaps of goat turd

This year fascists ascend the mountains
to recruit again from the villages

a lamb will accept even
the hardest rind of bread

—do I sing this?

40 years ago adults dress me as a cowgirl with a lisp

After they call the cave holy
people throw empty water bottles in it

when the lights go out the cowgirl
and I

freed from legibility

stop trying to boil the sadness out of
dandelion greens

One coral reef digests
its closest neighbor

another coral reef

PLASMA

I show up with my convincing accent and a middle-school vocabulary

my love of the sea, the sun, terraced hillsides, olive trees, the motorbike's
    tilt, luminous hunks of watermelon on a white plate, the same
    things tourists

imagine make them special

not precluding a quickly built hotel

a sewage treatment plant 2 km east of the popular beach

and I mean, you have to burn the garbage *some*where

with my haphazard grammar sprung from the refusal

to gender myself in a language

in which the requirement for being a person, for speaking—

we aren't precious about the sea when we stop to bathe on the return
    trip from Vathy

we aren't perfunctory either

we pull off at a small—you could call it a beach—you would never notice

in one motion you peel and fling your shirt

right next to the ring road

diagonal waves, minimal plastic

smooth dark stones huge as loaves of bread

walking on them stretches your foot soles

if unaccustomed it can hurt a bit

a gender neutral word for living creature is plasma

plasmata can do what people can't

a friend tells me

you have to shoo cats from the fish restaurant if you want to eat in peace

if you give them even one scrap

they don't leave you alone

when you look at a fence do you see the fence
when the slats are cut in the shape of a spear
or the shape of a new shoot in spring
can you tell the difference

your mother puts you in that red & white dress
and there are photos of it
are you inside the fence

when she sees her cousin
brought to the town square among the dead
"stacked in the bed of a wagon" she said

when the frantic hummingbird darts
in the field of tinsel in the grapevines shimmering
what is it you see

the surface of the water appears undisturbed
when more video evidence is released
a little surveillance device on the seat
mouthing off silently

a fraction of you still believed this could change the outcome

that the outcome can seem other than your life

a single night of back-to-back reality TV

you feel your atoms go by on the logging truck
carrying the strapped-down trunks of massive redwoods

throttling north

you see a woman bowing over a trashcan repeatedly and
she looks like she prays to—
Oh *help* her
          —! who made you think that

if no amount of "moving through the world with love"

when even armies think themselves beautiful
or so you are told

if all the daily errands drown it out
does it have a name

when border agents empty gallons onto the desert floor
on camera while smiling

when weighing whether or not to repeat this what do you consult

watching red berries on a bush shake, and a red robin shit,
and the red brake lights of a Prius on a turn

when a low plane combs the birds from their treetops
your thoughts scatter
to their familiar positions

if numbed now by emphasis
are you inside it

when fisherfolk "agree" to saw their boats in half
for a one-time payment (cash)

green opalescent feathers are green opalescent feathers
artists who design border wall prototypes are artists
who say they "leave politics out of it"

you trace the shape of those words in your mouth

red tips of matches
red tips of drought-tolerant succulents

a garden hose coiled on a wooden post
continents away

you try to separate pain from its subject
you try to separate yourself from its cause

while a man in cowboy pants declares
the greatness of George Bush

you stack electronic gems one atop the next

and of course he is a donor

by remaining in the building
you become what the building contains

the joint in a polished oak bench
the exhausted cloth applying the polish

when by fucking so hard
you try to make your body reappear

are you inside the fence
when

you saw your neighbor keeping her head down
and wondered if you should keep your head down

you heard your neighbor screaming in the street
and knew you should also scream

self-proclaimed
self-worth

self-restrained
self-love

self-watering
self-image

self-conscious
self-interest

self-limiting
self-starter

self-titled
self-obsession

self-indulgent
self-transcendence

self-punishing
self-mastery

self-locking
self-discovery

self-disciplined
self-mockery

self-reliant
self-blame

self-satisfied
self-examination

self-employed
self-deception

self-medicated
self-acceptance

self-congratulatory
self-censorship

self-appointed
self-respect

self-centered
self-contempt

self-loading
self-abnegation

self-defeating
self-help

self-serving
self-sabotage

self-adhesive
self-regard

self-certified
self-criticism

self-soothing
self-absorption

self-diagnosed
self-pity

selfless
self-storage

self-governed
self-loathing

self-published
self-assessment

self-stimulating
self-defense

self-fulfilling
self-deprivation

self-care
selfie

selfish
self-hatred

self-destructive
self-promotion

self-aware
self-denial

self-healing
self-checkout

self-repressed
self-repression

self-sealing
self-possession

self-monitored
self-confidence

self-regulating
self-portrait

self-canceling
self-justification

selfsame
selfhood

self-reflexive
self-delusion

self-deprecating
self-service

self-policed
self-perception

self-adjusting
self-esteem

self-cleaning
self-doubt

self-financed
self-righteousness

self-protective
self-forgetting

WE DON'T DRIVE TO THE SEA BUT
WE TALK ABOUT THE SEA

Rain laid into my grimy windowpane at an angle,

a cocky guy against a car waiting waiting.

To watch water magnify the screen's perfect squares

then extinguish, like lights in an office building

after hours when cleaning crews come in and leave.

From my desk I study it where

I take my little peasant meal, poached egg brown bread white cheese

grapefruit juice brief and dense.

A "peasant meal" though the bread was $7 the eggs too

and purchased while in the luxury of a bad mood.

No peasants write poems some asshole says

and that asshole is me.

If one notion follows another the sense I make

will break itself against itself.

Round white petals on the street I think are shattered glass

I steer around while they flutter then go still.

A baby carrot in a bag of baby carrots nuzzled

and shaved down into this wet shape why

so it could be forgotten so it wouldn't have to be itself.

Who wants to read about flower petals

who wants to read about all the theory you've read.

This blessed juice is sour and real.

On that part of the island
where the ruined tanneries beside the seawall conduct
their own inner lives
you tried like a fetishist of the broken
to photograph the sky through their vacant ceilings
but none of the blue would hold still in its frames while
onto the cellophane snack bags
blown into corners and a few
resplendent sunbleached cans you projected
a prefabricated sorrow
you know better than to say aloud
the blue's tirelessness is a selling point
so insistent it scalds
and against all proportion your dollars
materialize another carafe of chilled white
full of undisclosed feeling
crushed in the common barrel and
so light on the tongue you think it fated
that's the kind of lie you like
barely effervescent, unattributed
a note of ache in the semen
shot into the dirt outside the discotheque
painted tourist pink with a classical name
you gesture again to the filched marble
the headless goddess
dickless youth
they each seem to be you!
clinging to absence
like some backstage pass to the afterlife
not asking how your nose

how your knowledge
got that pitch
as you ride it down into the guts of the myth
immortal pyramid scheme
still coining itself in your lens
a little shroud made only of sunlight
only of sunlight and the chewed
quarter rind of watermelon balanced
on a cement post
at a construction project paused
for mismanagement of funds

it is easy to use a word
like "breathtaking"

to describe the idea
but not the feeling

of water you don't touch

you stand on a bluff
watching cargo ships slide on it

in mid-size port towns with no tourists
starving cats see it sparkling like this

from the other side of his life it sparkles
next to the cement plant next to the waste processing facility

four kilometers away a chain of cafés and an ouzeri
with narrow cane-bottomed chairs that hurt your ass overlook it

on windy days the whitecaps resemble distant sheep

from the yard it's new each time she sees it

a phrase at the tip of her mind she meant to say, did she already say
like little sheep? but today it sparkles

until conditions change it sparkles like this

officials don't mention it

when they cite the bounds of territorial waters
to prohibit a rescue boat from docking

in their personal libraries
some of the poetry describes it catching light

it is easy to imagine

using certain phrases
avoiding others
to deflect what doesn't sparkle like this

it is easy
to imagine a poem recited at a future occasion

in honor of a donor
or a dead politician

where you can be sure
from most angles the water will

They paid them to cut their olive trees down.

You paid them to cut their olive trees down.

We paid them to cut their olive trees down.

They paid you to cut your olive trees down.

We paid you to cut our olive trees down.

They paid you to cut their olive trees down.

We paid them to cut our olive trees down.

They paid us to cut their olive trees down.

They paid us to cut your olive trees down.

We paid you to cut their olive trees down.

We paid them to cut your olive trees down.

You paid them to cut our olive trees down.

You paid us to cut our olive trees down.

We paid you to cut your olive trees down.

They paid us to cut our olive trees down.

WASTE

a piece of pleated gold wrapping from a poinsettia
in yesterday's downpour

caught and rode the gushing current
downhill

it stalled between curb and parked cars

followed by an ebullient orange
bounding through the gray

free

the orange exited the narrative

we have more work to do

this morning the gold thing
still hanging around next to a parked car
like a big empty flower or a loud hat

lightly stirring not pinned

I remember two ladies from Saint Margaret Mary
carrying wilted poinsettias to the trash on a windy day

the gold is joined by a purple ball of tissue
resembling one of those horrible plastic shower poofs

our purpose is not what they told us our purpose is

My view has a sooty cathedral in it.
Often I pass a fountain
with the face of a merman
about to spit water through
chipped lower lip but
holding it in. There will be
another postcard rack.
Another stall at the market
displaying African wax prints
on tote bags, dresses, broad skirts
sold by a white man. I copy a list
of French colonies and their dates
into a blank white notebook.
On a bed of ice lay
haphazard piles of silver-gray fish. "The eye
should be clear," said my mother.
I don't want to look
at the eye. What's visible
from inside a Brutalist building.
Institutional green
linoleum tiles c. 1961, of a sturdy kind
the year my mother emigrates.
What's visible alongside
the nearly motionless canal.
Alongside a river
brownish-green, predictable,
like a few-weeks fling
that soon splits in two directions.
Irrepressible bodies of water
surrounded by buildings from centuries prior

whose filigrees gather soot
as excess definition.
Wreathed in trash
something classical
and repulsive endures.
The exterior of the famous museum
once a fortress
is power washed
behind large scaffolds fitted with tarps
screenprinted to mimic
the exterior of the famous museum.
One vertical band of newly washed portion
bare and ridiculous beside the
car-crammed thoroughfare. Piss
against trees and walls and the seams where walls meet
trickles and stinks like a moat.
In a concavity where the likeness
of another wealthy person once stood
pigeons sit.
The oxidized face
of a statue of some goddess
streaked in it.
In the gay club the dancer showers in front of us live
behind glass coyly
not revealing his dick
while screens project him digitized
in slight distortion on either side of him.
He snaps a small white towel
in front of himself and keeps it up
against the glass with his own weight.
Under this dancefloor
across from the bathrooms
a red room cordoned off.

It doesn't have to be there to be there.
At the market's end
split tomatoes, nectarines
so soft they're left for free.

HUMAN TIME

Beige building with
black mildew streaking
down the side

Shut blinds above a
kitchen sink I
know is there

A plastic bottle
of luminous dish soap

its hourglass
at half

Succulents' small utterances

Faint gloom

You dissecting a crow
in science class
years ago

Someone with a clipboard
outside the market
asking for signatures

A cloud and a plane
pulled in opposite directions

Someone pushing me
up against a locker

cool
orange metal
at my shoulders

On the sunlit album cover
a price sticker

almost touching
the folk singer's
pinched brow

Two chairs
at the table
sit together

proxies for us

in human time
we're still outside of

Between each hour
and the next

are days
we take cover in
like roadside brush

I pressed
with my fingers
to "see"

A limp little forest
trying to remain
upright

Isn't rigidity a number's job

the blanket's job
to be sad

The white t-shirt's anonymity

In a room more chicken coop than room
I rent a fan that feels on my face like sound. Low traffic
from San Fernando, street named for a king who
became a city, a valley, a saint.
We are meant to repeat his name. Instead
I say *prickly pear*, a cactus
which spreads its many-paddled hands
into the space around itself. No pears.
I call Mom to ask what the latest austerity measures mean.
Some ants on the wall make their way from one
unseeable point to another; the banks have closed.
I tell her to barter; barter what, she says.
An acquaintance posts "Tourism:
The Best Way to Be an Ally to Greece"
as if each tourist's pleasure hosts
a charity. Mules clabber down the stone paths
loaded with grapes to make next year's wine,
if the tourists come back
next year, and we hope they will. I say we,
but I'm closer to they. Living temporarily
in a neighborhood named for the happy, who were
who exactly?
I grow a little stiff with, a little lean with, a little faint with, a little
worn with seeming.
I must need to conquer my mind.
The roses dead because of drought
because whoever lives here cares enough
to let their roses die. I must
need to conquer the notion
anything needs conquering.

Something in me can't tell
what belongs. The ants
for whom anything is a street.
What sounded like a gate opening
was eucalyptus branches dragging themselves along the tin roof.
A yellow butterfly that has no interest in me.
I have no interest in kings.

THE STEPPING PLACE

I remember little of the desert but the desert nursed me

A cool pink shadow hawk-shaped

flashed on the mountains

In the rented yard I pressed my forehead on a sliding door

while the rest of me floated

some inches off the ground

Neighbors in exercise clothes

watered their driveways

and the babysitter emptied a 2 liter 7UP

over my head

After lunch we crossed the street

to the edge of arid sprawl

surely condos now

How to name what conspired to make a settler out of me

the tempered car window between me and

not-me selling lollipops on the bridge

arranged in small cardboard trays

An opening in traffic would sweep the car forward

the shape of my father's relief

A larger feeling began to collect then

no lullaby could disperse

Not crying was the point

the point was continuing at an unbroken pace

Teacher combed the knots from my hair with gentle persistence

A feral tangle of string and wire

intricate, unmistakable

I found on some pipes attached to the house

told me to drag it around

I unhitched it

and it's that tangle I serve

4

In the spongy crack of

an Athens sidewalk

I find an opaque yellow marble

scuffed by life

I rinse

when I would rather

put it in my mouth

I make notches in the

stupid calendar

by which we measure

our apartness

the closed white back

of the building opposite

the mirrored

courthouse windows

that butt up against

all the city

that exists beyond

a well-dressed couple

entering the building

in soft blue and sharp white

who own hotels

my tongue who runs

from me in the patchwork ruins

is English

a walkway above

the sidewalk

in need of repair

refusal

from high offices

elsewhere on the Continent

I scavenge

plaster replicas

for lost nouns

so I can say more than

αυτό

Then the klarino begins

whose player strolls the residential blocks

looking up through the trees

a textured emotion you'll have

understood as also yours

before you heard it

in absence

I break into my constituent

parts

and in each one I love you

I gather stray coins

wrap them in paper

drop them through the trees

toward the sound

toward the street

———————

in the same spot

every day the discreet tin

of what was fish once

congealed in its corners

the center tongued clean

by cats who look like dirty ropes

I wanted to cradle my love's face

a resurgence of clouds bore down

I wanted them to cradle mine

everywhere the letters of

commercial signage jammed with spikes

no place to perch

to the sidewalk I bring my hot slush of feeling

someone glares at my legs like they get

in the way of his eyes

on a stair you smoke

belongings cinched beside you

you are said to be in the way

asleep in a doorway

the cup near your face so as to hear

anything placed in it

anything taken

all morning waiting for it to rain

then waiting for it to clear

under a canopy

beside a thick cement pillar

———————————

at ground level a worker washes

the government building's

tinted triple-paned glass

his long pole a series of poles

that bows under the mop head

with odd grace

water splatters the concrete that

satisfying music like the music of rugs

being beaten

of rinsing hot cement with a hose

in the cone of our attention

last night in a dark green dress

and red lipstick the singer looked pointedly

at someone in the third row

then up to the balcony

her hand on her chest

though engineered

the glance still electric I felt

first irritation, then pleasure

then irritation again

soapy water in a normal red bucket

the government's filthy

mop water

before the

windows gleamed and now

they still gleam

———

we leave a lush salad out

on the streetside café table at midnight

fleeing from teargas

I cough in the bathroom

someone in Greek: hey light a cigarette would you?

someone in English: now you've had an authentic experience

———

don't be sorry for the future sand

this stone wall will become

don't be sentimental

about what's functional

(i.e., that dull steak knife

with speckled brown plastic handle

from Mama's first

American host family

in the kitchen drawer)

lodged between the wall's gray boulders

a huge white quartz

someone has painted a blue circle on

to guard against the evil eye

who here is blue-eyed?

on the path I find again

the ram's skull camouflaged in dry brush

the heads of bathers above water

abandoned terraces

that only seem abandoned

two systems of thought

we'll get there and we won't

platitudes like stupid bows on groomed dogs

on babies

who put everything in their mouths

let the paper disintegrate

the head of John the Baptist painted

in the mountain chapel

rosy-lipped as a cherub

on a modest canvas

beside the stack of candles to light

to honor our departed

Will says he's interested in pain

as a formal feature

in the relation between words

and phrases

so

can I cut my hair with this knife?

―――――

as the stout mini-fridge churns

in my bare hotel room

I smash a cockroach with an empty water bottle

second life

third life

against marble

nothing has a chance

though locally famous

they locked the sculptor in the asylum

apart from his statues

his mind cooled by marble

―――――

I want to send a video of you

to the water

as though the water could receive it

―――――

The way you go toward yourself

is a door that keeps opening

it widens

the vapor a small boat makes

ocean lard

fans out in all directions

from this bleached island

shirred sea

what isn't the center of the world

if the world has no center

the stroke

the eye

the holes

the point

the expanse reflecting

itself and not

a brief fish

netted

partly recovered

the sweat of a horse

the wet of its eye

the last bit of holy ghost

in hell

in whose suburb we live

Here I stop

the clink of spoon on cup

an argument audible through the wall

and this wind that slaps the sea

indiscreetly

another court ruling

"handed down"

one can clear their throat repeatedly and it won't clear

blue so dark it's purple

and therefore silver

The spoon stirs a two-note song

atrocities with names

I don't want to repeat

The sickness of a word

animating its referent

when its referent is death

the rash I suffered as a child in patches

has appeared on my hand again the one

I write and fuck and cut and grab

and touch you with

Will I have acted recklessly when asked

"where were you during that time?"

I was writing a poem

that had no body

I was blockading a detention facility

with my mind

I was on an island

stirring coffee with a mini spoon

inflammation echoing inside me

I was an oil slick on the Aegean

shattered particles of plastic lacing the surface

I held keys to the room I was locked in

the paint flaked

a great crack spanned it

the wall stood

for the time being

we sought shelter in the structures crumbling

one lived the next twenty years in a state

of shock and immobilizing heartbreak

one fell in love and bought a house

in a neighborhood of bureaucrats and cops

how many laws now against well-being

against simply being

and elemental as we are

we have a nervous breakdown

the fences will come to their knees

metals cease to cooperate

a hinge where there wasn't

powder where solid

the jail sink with the jailers

the empty cells

and the air itself

inescapable

I was still writing then

uneven braid of disbelief and belief

I described that portion of the sea

and the slope of patient mustard-brown land

destroyed

still living

lunar   picked clean

I could see

NOTES

TIME LAPSE

"boil the sadness out of dandelion greens" owes a debt to Jenny Mastoraki's *ΔΙΟΔΙΑ (TOLL)*. Kedros, 1972:

> the way steam escaping
> from the kettle lid
> takes with it
> part of the legume's ache
> and the wild dandelion's bitterness.

(translation mine)

MEANDER/ΜΑΙΑΝΔΡΟΣ

The Meander or Menderes is a river in what is present-day Turkey. Aesthetically, the meander refers to an ancient design motif made from a continuous line and named after this winding river, commonly seen in Greek vase painting and architecture.

SPECTRA

"ardent sun" is from Etel Adnan's *Of Cities and Women (Letters to Fawwaz)*. The Post-Apollo Press, 1993.

"like a Palmyra matron / Copied in lard and horsehair" is from James Merrill's poem "Days of 1964," in *Nights and Days*. Atheneum, 1966.

"exhausted blue" is from James Merrill's *The (Diblos) Notebook*. Dalkey Archive, 1994.

"imagine the whole country is a museum . . . every little stone" was said by Nikolas Kosmatopoulos at Πραξεις Ανυπακοής IV \\ Acts of Disobedience IV, a discussion with Decolonize This Place hosted by 1927 Art Space on April 8, 2021.

PRONOUN STUDY

I'm indebted to Helen Dimos for the originating phrase, and to her father and her sister's godfather Andreas, for confirming the anecdote about incentives the EU paid to farmers in Crete in the 1980s to clear agricultural land of olive trees and plant grape vines instead.

ACKNOWLEDGMENTS

Thank you to the land where I live and work, Huchiun (Oakland), the unceded homeland of the Ohlone people. As a settler here, I support nothing less than the return of this land to the Ohlone, and the return of all Indigenous lands to Indigenous peoples.

Thank you to Ben Estes and Alan Felsenthal of The Song Cave for publishing portions of this book in a 2018 chapbook also titled *A Symmetry*. Grateful acknowledgment is made to the editors of *Ambit*, *BathHouse Journal*, *The Georgia Review*, *Hyperallergic*, *Jewish Currents*, *Kenyon Review*, *The Nation*, *The New Republic*, *PLI (Pour une Littérature Incendiaire)*, *Poetry*, *A Public Space*, *The Rumpus*, *Washington Square Review*, and *The Yale Review*, where a number of these poems first appeared, sometimes in earlier versions.

Gratitude to John DeWitt and Lise Thiollier, and to Sudden Darling, for translating some of these poems into French and Greek, respectively. Thank you to Diane Seuss, who selected an excerpt from the manuscript for the 2019 Alice Fay Di Castagnola Award, and to the late Kevin Killian, who selected "Curriculum" for the 2019 Cecil Hemley Memorial Award, and whose capacious life and work remain a marvel.

For constellations of time, space, and material resources, gratitude to Cité Internationale des Arts, Headlands Center for the Arts, Lighthouse

Works, MacDowell, the 2018 Paros Translation Symposium, and the people who labor to make these spaces possible. Gratitude to Tyler Schnoebelen for use of the big desk under the redwoods.

Thank you to my editor Jill Bialosky, to Drew Weitman, and all at Norton for their support and attentiveness in bringing this book into its physical form.

Thank you to Zoe Leonard for permission to reproduce the photograph on the cover, for what your seeing makes seen.

Thank you to my colleagues and students for all you share with me.

Ana Božičević, Gregg Bordowitz, Brandon Shimoda, Eleni Sikelianos, and Asiya Wadud, immense gratitude for the care of your words, here and elsewhere. Special thanks to this manuscript's (and this life's) readers: Kerry Carnahan, Maxe Crandall, Ghazal Mosadeq, Margaret Ross, Charif Shanahan, Solmaz Sharif, and Brandon Som, who each offered vital insights, and friendship which has sustained me more variously and profoundly than I can express here. Thank you: for your joyous example of presence, Suzanne Gardinier; for your insistence on precision, Louise Glück; for pointing me to Katerina Gogou before I knew I needed her, Eleni Bourou. For provocations, energies, and companionship that fed the making, gratitude to Samuel Ace, Wilder Alison, Jen Bervin, Julian Talamantez Brolaski, Diana Cage, Sara Cooper, Helen Dimos, Valentine Freeman, Gabriela Garcia, Jenny Johnson, Aditi Khorana, Candice Lin, Trisha Low, Naomi Mulvihill and Jessie Auger, Leah Pires, the Poliak-Smith family, Cooper Sabatino, Monica Sok, Syd Staiti, Sara Jane Stoner, Öykü Tekten, Alli Warren, Anna Martine Whitehead, and Sasha Wortzel.

To my parents, Irene and Pandelis,
to Aleksei, Solmaz, and mara,
an infinity. The radiant sun.